Asking Questions abo...

Asking Questions About How Hollywood Movies Get Made

Jan Fields

Published in the United States of America by Cherry Lake Publishing
Ann Arbor, Michigan
www.cherrylakepublishing.com

Consultants: Sam Fischer, Director, Samfischer LLC; Marla Conn, ReadAbility, Inc.
Editorial direction and book production: Red Line Editorial
Book design: Sleeping Bear Press

Photo Credits: Lakeview Images/Shutterstock Images, cover, 1; iStockphoto, 5, 6, 10; Dick Johnson CC 2.0, 9; Warner Brothers/Everett Collection, 15; Scott Ehardt, 17; S. Bukley/Shutterstock Images, 19; Everett Historical/Shutterstock Images, 21; Jordan Strauss/Invision/AP Images, 22; Fuse/Thinkstock, 25; Ed Stock/iStockphoto, 27; Frank Trapper/Corbis, 28

Copyright © 2016 by Cherry Lake Publishing
All rights reserved. No part of this book may be reproduced or utilized in
any form or by any means without written permission from the publisher.

Library of Congress Cataloging-in-Publication Data

Fields, Jan.
  Asking questions about how Hollywood movies get made / by Jan Fields.
     pages cm. -- (Asking questions about media)
  Includes bibliographical references and index.
  ISBN 978-1-63362-488-7 (hardcover : alk. paper) -- ISBN 978-1-63362-504-4 (pbk. : alk. paper) -- ISBN 978-1-63362-520-4 (pdf ebook) -- ISBN 978-1-63362-536-5 (hosted ebook)
  1. Motion pictures--United States--History and criticism--Juvenile literature. I. Title.
  PN1993.5.U6F465 2015
  791.430973--dc23
                                           2015005523

Cherry Lake Publishing would like to acknowledge the work of
the Partnership for 21st Century Skills. Please visit *www.p21.org*
for more information.

Printed in the United States of America
Corporate Graphics Inc.

ABOUT THE AUTHOR

Jan Fields is a teacher, writer, and passionate film fan. She has written more than 20 books for young people, both fiction and nonfiction. With a passion for storytelling and action, she just might try writing a screenplay of her own someday!

TABLE OF CONTENTS

CHAPTER 1
The Magic of Movies 4

CHAPTER 2
The Green Light 8

CHAPTER 3
Movies and Messages 14

CHAPTER 4
Challenges and Changes 20

CHAPTER 5
Building an Audience 24

THINK ABOUT IT 30
LEARN MORE 31
GLOSSARY 32
INDEX 32

The Magic of Movies

An audience gathered at the Grand Café in Paris, France, in 1896. They came to watch *Arrival of the Train* by Louis Lumière. The movie lasted only 50 seconds. It showed a train pulling into a station. The black-and-white images flickered on the screen. The noisy projector was the only sound in the room. The train chugged straight at the camera. The audience gasped.

Movie audiences still gasp, laugh, cry, and scream during movies. The power of movies to thrill audiences hasn't changed much. But the way these films are made

Movies have been entertaining us for more than 100 years.

certainly has changed. The first movies were recordings of everyday events. Over time, people began using movies to tell stories. The stories became more complicated. So did the methods used to tell them.

Early filmmakers experimented with new ways to use the camera to capture a story. Inventors gave filmmakers better tools. Movies began being made with sound. Then color filming became the norm. Tools continued to become more sophisticated. Today, Hollywood movies are made with both cameras and

Cameras, lights, and computers are just some of the tools used to shoot movies.

computers. Storytelling is done with live actors, animated characters, or both.

For the filmmaker, every step of the film's creation involves questions. What kind of message will the movie share? What technology will be used? Where will the money for making the movie come from? Movie viewers can dig deeper into this world by asking questions of their own:

- Who decides which films are made in Hollywood?
- Who influences a movie's message?
- How have the messages in Hollywood movies changed over time, and why?
- How does Hollywood convince viewers to watch?

We'll explore these questions and more as we look at how Hollywood movies are made.

It Takes a Village

The Motion Picture Association of America (MPAA) reports that the film industry supports nearly 2 million workers. Most of these people are never seen on the screen. Directors guide the actors' performances. Writers create and revise the screenplay. Designers plan sets and costumes. Filmmaking also includes very practical jobs. Movies need accountants to keep track of all the costs of the film. Wardrobe staff prepare actors' clothing. Electricians keep lights working safely. Drivers carry actors and other crew members to the set. All these people and more work to make movies happen.

The Green Light

The marquee at your local theater probably gives you many viewing options. But who decides which films are made?

Before the first scene is shot, important decisions are made about the movie. This is the time of development and preproduction.

In development, a writer may base a screenplay on a book or an original idea. A director could raise money to turn a story into a movie. A studio executive could like a concept and hire the people to make it into a movie. No matter where the idea comes from, the process of deciding if that idea will make a good movie is complex.

The idea must first become a story on paper. The first writing of the story might be very short. It outlines the plot of the movie. This is called a treatment.

Marvel Studios' Avengers *franchise has been a hit around the world and produced numerous sequels and spinoffs.*

Sometimes more detail is needed to decide if the story is worth turning into a movie. A longer version of a treatment is a screenplay. This screenplay may be rewritten many times before it becomes a movie.

Finally, the idea reaches the point of calling a "green-light" meeting. In this meeting, a Hollywood studio decides whether to make the movie—to give it the "green light," or go-ahead to start filming. There may be 30 or 40 people at one of these meetings. They must consider the business side of the project equally or more than the creative side. How much will the movie cost to make? Where will it be filmed?

Some movies benefit from product tie-ins, like this Rapunzel doll from Disney's Tangled.

How many actors are needed? Will there be many computer effects? Are there possible product tie-ins, such as children's toys?

Movies can cost more than $100 million to make, so filmmakers are always looking for ways to reduce the risk of a movie failing. One way is to make movies that build on ideas that have already been successful. *Harry Potter and the Half-Blood Prince* and *Spider-Man 3* were **sequels** to popular movies. *Tangled* became part of the highly successful Disney princess movies. Most princess movies draw large audiences.

Marvel Success

When Marvel Studios began making movies based on its superhero comics, something amazing happened. The movie franchise became one of the most successful in Hollywood history. The studio made $6.1 billion for its first eight films. This success meant Marvel could green-light more movies far earlier than usual. As a result, more than 20 movies based on their comic book universe have been made or were scheduled for production by 2019.

There are other ways to reduce risk too. Hollywood makes movies based on popular novels, comic books, and video games. It produces remakes of movies or television shows that were successful years ago. Remakes draw in people who loved the original film or show. They might bring in new audiences who are unfamiliar with the original. Another way to reduce the risk of a movie failing is to cast popular actors. All of these choices help produce films with less financial risk.

The Spider-Man character spawned a successful series of movies.

Case Study
The Princess Bride

Some movies take a long time to make. William Goldman wrote *The Princess Bride* as a story for his kids in the early 1970s. A studio executive at 20th Century Fox liked the book and was interested in turning it into a movie. Goldman wrote a screenplay for the studio. Then the studio executive that liked the book lost his job. The new executive at the studio didn't want to make the old executive's movies. But Goldman didn't give up.

Executives at other studios liked Goldman's book, but something always seemed to stand in the way of it becoming a movie. Two more executives who wanted to turn the book into a movie were fired. Another studio closed the weekend before it planned to begin work on the film. Years passed. Goldman wondered if his book would ever be a movie. Finally Rob Reiner, a Hollywood director who had read and loved the book, decided to make the film and was able to see it through.

After it was finished, *The Princess Bride* was difficult to market. The story combines fantasy, action, comedy, and romance. No one knew how to make a good **trailer** for it. Should the trailer be funny? Should it show action? The movie saw limited success when it was released in theaters in 1987—not many people went to see it. But those who did see the film loved it. Through word of mouth praising it, the movie sold well on home video. Today *The Princess Bride* is considered a true classic.

[Asking Questions about Media]

CHAPTER 3

Movies and Messages

Movies tell stories and provide entertainment. They can also contain messages, or hidden meanings. Often those messages result in **controversy**. Some critics complained that the movie *The Iron Giant* had an antigun message. Others said *The Incredibles* warns of the danger of pointless lawsuits. *WALL-E* is an animated movie set in a world destroyed by **consumerism**. Who does the movie blame for this destruction? Some critics think the movie is antibusiness. Different viewers see the content differently. But who influences the messages the movies send?

Movie messages often reflect the beliefs of the movie's director. The messages often stem from the **culture** of the time at which they are made. For example, a common movie conflict involves a struggle between the weak and the powerful. The powerful characters are often villains. Villains might be powerful because they are strong, or because they have a lot of money. In some movies, the powerful foe is a big business or people who are destroying the environment. For instance, in *Cars 2*, the oil industry is the

Some critics thought The Iron Giant *had an antigun message.*

Once a little-known candy, Reese's Pieces got a huge bump in popularity when it was featured in E.T. the Extra-Terrestrial.

villain. The conflict centers on the use of oil, which pollutes the environment when used for energy, versus alternative fuels that do not. These issues were important to the public at the time the movies were made.

A director's choices can be influenced by outside forces in surprising ways. In the movie *E.T. the Extra-Terrestrial*, filmmakers planned to show a scene where the alien eats the candy Milk Duds. Later in the movie, the alien gets sick. The makers of Milk Duds worried viewers would think their candy made the alien sick.

They turned down the chance to be in the movie. Instead the film featured a candy that was newer at the time, called Reese's Pieces. Being in the film resulted in huge sales of that candy. Today, companies often pay filmmakers to have their products shown in movies.

Studios also might make changes based on a test-audience reaction. A test audience sees a rough version of a movie. Then they answer questions. They tell what they liked and didn't like about the movie. Because of the reactions of a test audience, *E.T. the Extra-Terrestrial* changed. In the rough film, the alien character died. The test audience didn't like the sad ending. They

PASSING THE TEST

Director Ron Howard finds audience testing useful for discovering areas that confuse or upset an audience. But he admits the process is hard. "I mean, the whole preview experience is not fun. Even when it's going well, it's not fun. You never want to be proven to be mistaken about anything," he said.

wanted him to live and find his way back home. A new final cut gave the film this happy ending.

Remakes sometimes offer a filmmaker a chance to change or add to the movie's message. For instance, a remake might reflect more **diversity** than the original. *The Wizard of Oz* was released in 1939. In 1975, it was reimagined as a stage play called *The Wiz*. The play had a largely African-American cast and more modern music. The popularity of this Broadway musical resulted in a movie version in 1978.

ANNIE REMAKE

The classic musical *Annie* has traditionally starred a Caucasian girl with bright red curls. When African-American actress Quvenzhané Wallis was cast for the remake in 2014, online comments included a number of negative reactions to the changes in casting. But the filmmakers didn't change the cast in response. They thought the negative feedback was racist and not worth their attention.

Actress Quvenzhané Wallis was cast as the title character in the 2014 remake of Annie.

Challenges and Changes

The first moving pictures simply captured everyday life. When films began to tell stories, they also shared messages. How have those messages changed over the years?

Audiences don't always buy into a movie's message. In 1940, Charlie Chaplin's comedy *The Great Dictator* tried to draw attention to the suffering of the Jews in Europe during World War II (1939–1945). The United States had not yet entered the war. And many

In the 1930s groups such as the Legion of Decency pushed filmmakers to restrict adult content in movies.

Americans wanted it to stay that way. As a result, the movie received much criticism.

People began to worry about the content in movies, too. Some thought movies were too violent or made bad behavior appear to be acceptable. In the 1930s, groups formed to push for government **censorship** of movies. The Catholic Church formed the Legion of Decency. It pressured filmmakers to restrict content the church considered inappropriate.

[ASKING QUESTIONS ABOUT MEDIA]

Steve McQueen shows off the Oscar he won for directing 12 Years a Slave.

Filmmakers knew they had to act or the government would pass laws restricting movie content. The movie studios created the Production Code Administration (PCA) in 1934. The PCA forced movies to follow a set of rules called the Production Code. The code covered depictions of violence, criminal activity, and sex. It also said movies had to support America and democracy.

Over time, filmmakers began to resist PCA rules. Foreign films and strong independent films grew more popular. These films did not follow the code. It became clear that audiences wanted movies that were more realistic. Filmmakers pushed back against the rules. The variety of films being produced grew.

Today, Hollywood films reflect the things that concern Americans now. Films such as the comedy *Barbershop* deal with diversity issues. Disney's *Mulan* and *Brave* show girls pushing against the rules of society. Environmental messages are also popular today. *Happy Feet* shows how pollution and overfishing endanger the animals of the antarctic region.

HOLLYWOOD DIVERSITY

One way film has changed today is the inclusion and depiction of women and racial minorities. White men once dominated the film industry. Today, filmmaking is open to women and minorities. In 2010, Kathryn Bigelow became the first woman to win the **Oscar** for best director. And in 2013, Steve McQueen became the first African-American director to win the Oscar for best picture. This diversity brought new voices to filmmaking.

CHAPTER 5

Building an Audience

For a movie to succeed, audiences must see it, either in theaters or via DVDs and digital downloads. But how does Hollywood convince you to see a movie? Audience demand is created if people hear about the movie and like what they've heard. This is why Hollywood spends so much money on **publicity**. Studios have spent more than $50 million in advertising for major films. The ads run in the weeks just before the movie opens at theaters. Most of the publicity budget is spent on television ads.

Television has proven to be the best way to reach the most people.

A movie's trailer is an important part of its advertising budget. The trailer is like a tiny film about the movie. It must be short and exciting. It needs to get the audience's attention and cause an emotional reaction to the movie. Trailers can take months to make. They

Hollywood knows that children have a lot of influence over the products their parents buy.

CASE STUDY
TRANSFORMERS TIE-INS

Along with television advertising, some promotion is tied to products that are popular with the film's intended audience. The studio DreamWorks wanted children to see the movie *Transformers*. So it partnered with restaurant chain Burger King to sell 25 million *Transformers* kids meals. DreamWorks also teamed with Kraft Foods on 25 million *Transformers* Lunchables, which are prepackaged lunches. Children who ate those products would be exposed to the movie, so it was a good deal for DreamWorks. And kids who knew of and liked the movie would be more likely to ask their parents to buy the movie-related food products. So it was a good deal for Burger King and Kraft Foods, too.

use a combination of music and visuals to make audiences excited about the film. Sometimes more than one trailer is made for the same movie. Trailers are used to advertise the movie on television, in theaters, and on the Internet.

When a movie's publicity campaign is successful, references to the movie will pop up on social media. When people talk about a movie, it's called "buzz." All filmmakers want buzz. Actors who star in the movie usually play a part in building buzz. They appear on talk shows and interact with fans directly through social media. When a movie has buzz, ticket sales soar.

Movie stars usually agree to help publicize their films by doing interviews and interacting with fans via social media.

[ASKING QUESTIONS ABOUT MEDIA]

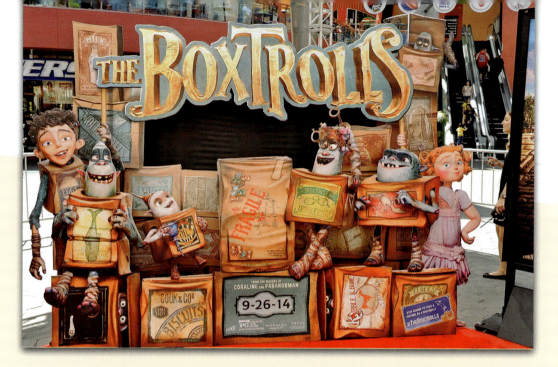

The MPAA monitors movie posters and lobby displays to ensure their content is appropriate for all ages.

Movie advertising is carefully monitored for the messages it sends. The MPAA makes sure ads display movie ratings. This helps audiences decide if a movie is appropriate for their age and interests. Movie ratings are based on content. In 1968, the first MPAA rating system was created. It rates movies based on how much adult content a film contains. Movies are rated G, PG, PG-13, R, and NC-17. A G movie contains nothing inappropriate for children. PG and PG-13 movies are best watched with parental guidance. Both R and NC-17 movies contain adult content that isn't appropriate for children.

The MPAA Advertising Administration also monitors images and words on movie posters and cardboard displays in theater lobbies. It watches for material that depicts adult content.

Movies have entertained people of all ages for more than 100 years, and they continue to be one of the most prominent forms of media. As you watch them, keep in mind all the steps it takes to get a movie to the theater or your living room. From choosing a script to convincing you to see the movie, there's a lot more to filmmaking than meets the eye.

DIGITAL MARKETING

In 1999, the makers of the movie *The Blair Witch Project* launched an Internet campaign. They posted movie clips online. They said the clips were from three young filmmakers who had disappeared while filming. People discussed online whether the clips were real. This buzz made the low-budget film a hit.

THINK ABOUT IT

Think about the advertising you see for a film. What is the movie company doing to make the film appealing to you?

Talk with friends who have seen a movie. Did they enjoy it? Why? Ask questions to learn more about what they liked or didn't like.

Think before you buy movie-related **merchandise**. Do you really want this item? How has advertising affected your desire for the product? Will you continue to want this long after the movie is forgotten?

When you watch a film, ask yourself what messages the movie presents. Do you agree with those messages? How does the movie affect your views?

LEARN MORE

FURTHER READING

Downing, Todd. *Master This! Filmmaking.* New York: PowerKids Press, 2011.

Horn, Geoffrey M. *Writing, Producing, and Directing Movies.* Berkeley Heights, NJ: Enslow, 2008.

O'Neill, Joseph R. *Cool Careers, Movie Director.* Ann Arbor, MI: Cherry Lake, 2010.

WEB LINKS

AFI.com: History of AFI
www.afi.com/about/history.aspx
Learn about the history of the American Film Institute.

Internet Movie Database
www.imdb.com
Read reviews, cast lists, and trivia about specific movies.

Motion Picture Association of America
www.mpaa.org
Find information about copyright, jobs, and changing film technology.

GLOSSARY

censorship (SEN-sur-ship) removing parts of a book, film, play, etc., thought to be harmful or offensive to the public

consumerism (cuhn-SOO-muh-rism) purchase, use, and discarding of goods desired by the population

controversy (CAHN-truh-vur-see) discussions reflecting strong and emotional differences in opinion about a subject

culture (KUHL-chur) customs, habits, and traditions of a society

diversity (duh-VUR-sit-ee) inclusion of a variety of different people and cultures

merchandise (MUR-chan-deyez) products related to a specific film such as toys or T-shirts

Oscar (OSS-cur) an award given each year by the Academy of Motion Picture Arts and Sciences to the best performance or production in many categories of filmmaking

publicity (puh-BLISS-eht-ee) something designed to attract public attention to a film

sequels (SEE-kwhuls) books or movies that continue the story of an earlier work

trailer (TRAY-lur) short film created to promote a movie

INDEX

Annie, 18

Bigelow, Kathryn, 23
Blair Witch Project, The, 29

E.T. the Extra-Terrestrial, 16–17

Goldman, William, 13

Howard, Ron, 17

Legion of Decency, 21
Lumière, Louis, 4

Marvel Studios, 11
McQueen, Steve, 23
Milk Duds, 16–17
MPAA, 7, 28–29

PCA, 22–23
Princess Bride, The, 13
publicity, 24–29

ratings, 28–29
Reese's Pieces, 17
Reiner, Rob, 13

Wallis, Quvenzhané, 18
Wiz, The, 18
Wizard of Oz, The, 18
World War II, 20